# College Green 1919

The outer row of trees was removed for road widening, and the inner row was removed just before World War II to make way for a green area in front of the new Council House, started pre-1939 and finished after the end of the war.

Taylors and Son moved to Queens Road, but are now no longer in Bristol. Still many busy shops leading to the bottom of Park Street, with the modern offices of Bristol City Council on the left.

# Park Street 1910

There are at least 17 horse-drawn vehicles in this view of Park Street, rivalling today for busy congestion. The hill is without the University tower, and shows the twin towers of the Blind School.

Shops with their Georgian facades, and modern shop blinds. The university tower dominates the skyline as it has done since 1924.

# Victoria Rooms and Queens Road, Clifton 1905

Showing the newly erected statue to commemorate the Boer War, and the Victoria Room's, enclosed with wall and railings. The early bus just showing "en route for the Clifton Suspension Bridge".

The Boer War statue still stands today, surrounded by busy traffic. The railings were removed to erect a statue and fountains to commemorate the death of Edward VII in 1911, formally opened by George V in 1913.

# Queens Road, Clifton 1912

Looking down toward the Victoria Rooms, at the junction with Richmond Terrace. The spire of St. Pauls Church can be seen between the trees.

Now, the basement areas under the houses are used as restaurants and business premises, but the Georgian terrace remains unchanged. Queens Court Flats in the middle distance.

# Whiteladies Road 1918

Looking towards Clifton Down Station and the tower of Tyndale Baptist Church. A Cart of Rocklight Lamp Oil is parked outside C.F. Billing, Undertakers.

Whiteladies Road is still recognisable today, only the Clifton Down Shopping Centre on the left having replaced smaller shops. Clifton Down Station is behind, connecting with Temple Meads and Severn Beach.

# Blackboy Hill 1905

Blackboy Hill looking towards Durdham Downs, although not the official name, the hill was named after the famous Blackboy Inn, which once stood across the top of the hill.

The old Chapel, top right, survives today as a fitness centre, the ornate lamp standards sadly missed. What would the ladies in the top picture make of rose's at £2.45 a bunch? Many shops survive, their upper stores recognisable.

# Clifton Suspension Bridge 1863

Taken from the top of the tower looking towards Leigh Woods, the roadway nearing completion. The Bridge was completed, and the opening Ceremony held on 8th December 1864.

From the Somerset Tower looking towards Clifton, the spire of Christ Church on the skyline.

# King Street 1916

Near the Waterfront at Welsh Back, when carts were one of the main forms of delivery. Shows the Llandoger Trow on the right. Note the elaborate lamp over the door to the public tavern. St. Thomas's Church just visible behind the dock-side warehouses.

The Llandoger with only three pointed gables, the other two having been destroyed in the 1939-45 war. Good views of St. Thomas's Church, with Temple Church on the skyline.

# Section of City Docks 1924

*Section of City Docks with Coastwise and Continental Lines.*

Described as Coastwise and Continental lines, the picture shows what a busy dockland area it once was, with many ships berthed on both quays. At this point the Froom enters the floating harbour.

The Warehouses are now used for leisure interests, exhibitions, shops and cafes. The boat on the left is a floating restaurant called Inn at the Quay, with the former Bush Warehouse on the opposite bank now an Arts Centre.

# Redcliffe Wharf 1907

A busy scene with many cargo ships unloading. The spires of All Saints, St. Nicholas, and Christ Churches are visible on the skyline, by Bristol Bridge.

The dockland area on the left, in Welsh Back, has been taken over by Leisure interests yachting and sports centre. Many warehouses on the right survive, and have been converted into flats, retaining their old warehouse frontage.

# General Hospital 1907

This view of the Hospital from Coronation Road shows the dome of the Hospital still in place. The movable bridge is at the entrance to Bathurst Basin, with lock gates which let water from the basin into the cut.

The Dome of the Hospital is now gone, having been destroyed during World War II. St. Mary Redcliffe's spire just showing behind the Hospital. The Dockmaster's house has been demolished, although the warehouse is still the same. The movable bridge is still there today, but the lock gates are gone, a wall has been built in their place, with mud and silt built up against it.

# Great Britain 1971

The wrecked deck of the Great Britain on her return to Bristol from the Falkland Islands.

The deck now fully re-built, showing the funnel in place.

# Great Britain, early 1971

Having returned to Bristol from the Falkland Islands, where she had lain as a storage hulk since being damaged by storms in 1886.

Now back in the dry dock where originally built and open to the public, the ship is being restored. As can be seen, the figurehead, rigging and funnel are completed.

# St. Peters Church, Hotwells 1910

Looking towards the junction of Jacobs Wells Road and Hotwells Road from Anchor Road. The church and Parish Hall have a footpath between them, connecting Hotwells with Clifton Wood. The sign is for the Public Baths, which were situated in Jacobs Wells Road.

The island is now a busy roundabout with mature trees. Modern flats predominate, and one block is named St. Peters House, after the former church.

# Redcliffe Hill 1908

St. Mary Redcliffe Church showing at top of the Hill, and shops running down both sides of the road. Note also the tram lines and the attractive design of the holders which carry the overhead cables for the trams. The famous faggot and pea shop, with the faggots bubbling away in the copper pan, was to the right of the picture.

The spire of St. Mary Redcliffe just showing behind the flats. The road is now a dual carriageway. On the left is the modern Phoenix Assurance building.

# East Street, Bedminster 1917

Looking from Bedminster Parade showing a thriving shopping area, when the horse and cart was the main form of transport for delivering goods. The large building is the W.D. & H.O. Wills factory, manufacturing cigarettes and tobaccos, which was built between 1901-07. The far end with the dome were the head offices, with the public clock above the delivery bay.

W.D. & H.O. Wills have now moved to new premises at Hartcliffe. The old facade has been retained, and the building has been converted into shops. A large superstore with ample car parking space is behind, with smaller shops with an arcade adjoining the main road. The clock still tells the time today.

# The Round House, Ashton Gate 1910

The Round House stands at the junction of Coronation Road and North Street, formerly an old toll house. An advert for Singer Sewing Machines hangs above one of the shops.

The junction retains the frontage of the Round House incorporated with modern flats either side. Some of the shops converted to a cafe and private use on the right.

# Cross Road, West Street, Bedminster 1920

Looking towards East Street with the junction of West Street, and the London Inn on the left. No traffic about, people able to stand in the middle of the road for a chat.

East Street is still a very busy shopping area, made easier by being relatively traffic free, open to buses and access for business only. The Midland Bank is still on the corner.

# Bishopsworth 1934

A tranquil village scene, looking down Church Road with its village shops.

The two buildings to the right, along with the shop have gone, modern houses and shops having taken their place. A mini-roundabout has been put on the junction, with its accompanying bollards and signs.

# St. Augustines Parade 1910

Looking along the left side of the centre, from College Green. Shows many shops towards Colston Street. The tram, No. 214, went to Hotwells from Brislington.

An office block now obscures the view of Colston Street. Road signs direct the flow of traffic, and the clock on the former Tramways Office is still a useful time check today.

# The Palace Theatre, Baldwin Street, 1911

THE PALACE THEATRE, BALDWIN STREET, BRISTOL.

Opened on Boxing Day in 1892 as a Music Hall, it later became the Gaumont Cinema. During the intervals, the patrons were entertained by an organist who rose from the orchestra pit.

The number of windows on the upper floor has been reduced, and the old ornate canopy has been removed, to be replaced by a modern version. The building is now used as a night club and dance hall.

# Baldwin Street 1908

James Bigwood, who traded both in the retail and wholesale of poultry and fish, then formed part of the market scene in Baldwin Street.

The buildings remain much unchanged, but the fish market is now behind Baldwin Street in St. Nicholas Street.

# Bristol Bridge 1904

Bristol Bridge.

Sailing ship harboured at the quayside at Welsh Back, with warehouses on the right. The bridge was widened in the late 19th century, the metal pillars visible in front of the old stone bridge, and the road in the background, Bridge Street was part of the busy heart of Bristols main shopping thoroughfare.

The shopping area was mainly destroyed by air raids during World War II, 1939-45, as was St. Peters Church, the shell of which, together with modern offices, adjoin what is now an open area called Castle Park. The warehouse buildings on the right beyond the bridge are still used by a Brewery.

# Bristol Bridge 1916

This view of Bristol Bridge, taken in 1916, shows the road with cobble stones and tram lines in place. The building with a dome on it was the E.S. & A. Robinson building, which was later demolished for DRG's new 15 Storey Office Block.

Today Bristol Bridge has completely changed, with all buildings demolished to be replaced by new office blocks. The ICL Building was built only a few years ago. The DRG Building behind was built in 1963 and was the first air conditioned building in Bristol. On the far side of the Bridge, on the left, is where the Courage Brewery is today.

# Victoria Street 1933

Looking towards Bristol Bridge, at the junction of Victoria Street and Temple Street, with the statue of Neptune in the centre, where it had been since 1872. The tram was on en route for Bushy Park, Totterdown, from Old Market and Hanham.

The Neptune Statue was moved to the Quay Head on the Centre in 1949. Many of the buildings were destroyed in early 1940's. Motor showrooms on the left, and All Saints Church just visible. More modern offices, screened by trees, on the right.

# High Street, Bristol, 1920's

HIGH STREET, BRISTOL.

Looking up towards Christ Church and the junction of Wine, Corn and Broad Streets. The corner of St. Nicholas' Church can be seen on the left, and the stationers, Scholastic, on the opposite corner.

Much devastated during air raids in World War II, little remains except the Churches. St. Nicholas has only the original walls remaining, now converted into a Museum and Brass Rubbing Centre. The new St. Nicholas House is on the corner of St. Nicholas Street.

# Dutch House, Corner of Wine Street and High Street, 1917

Built in the 17th century and used for many purposes including a Bank and Shops. Wine Street and High Street were busy shopping thoroughfares. Jones Department Store (building adjoining Dutch House to the left) is now Debenhams of the Horsefair.

The Dutch House was damaged during an air-raid on November 24th 1940, and demolished by soldiers three days later on the 27th November. Now the modern premises of the Bank of England occupies the corner, with modern buildings and Castle Park beyond.

# The Horsefair 1909

Looking towards St. James Barton, with St. James Park on the left. The small park on the right formerly the site of St. James Churchyard. It was used for many years, until the early 19th century, as a site for Fairs, with roundabouts and swings etc. Revived again in the 1880's.

The large department store, John Lewis, was built on the site of St. James Churchyard. Remains of the former burial ground were found when excavating the foundations of the store. A corner of St. James Park, surrounded by mature trees showing on the left, with a view of new offices facing the Horsefair roundabout.

# The Horsefair 1910

Looking towards St. James Church from the corner of Silver Street, with St. James Park enclosed by trees. The spire to the right belongs to the Welsh Congregational Church. The small building in the middle of the road was a cab stand for Bristol Tramway staff, the tram lines visible in the foreground.

St. James Church just visible through the trees, with the tree lined park next door. The Welsh Church was demolished in the 1950's for redevelopment. Now a modern office block has been built in its place, and the tall building behind is the headquarters of Avon County Council.

# Tower Hill 1924

Showing busy shops, either side of the road, with people walking by and men cleaning windows. The corner behind the tram is Old Market Street.

Today the scene has completely changed, with all old buildings having been demolished. Ambulance Station now on left and in middle distance is the Holiday Inn.

# Rupert Street and Quay Street, 1918

The Demerara Figurehead, a West African Chieftain, was saved from a ship that broke its back whilst on its maiden voyage in 1851, displayed above a shop of Auctioneers and Valuers. Fry's Chocolate Factory can be seen to the right of the figurehead.

The Fry's Chocolate Factory completed their move to Somerdale, Keynsham in 1934, the move having taken some 11 years, from the Central City site. The Demerara Figurehead was removed a few years earlier in 1931. Road widening occurred when Electricity House was built in 1938. Greyfriars Office building was built in the 1970's in Rupert Street, and more modern developments occurred in Nelson Street.

# South Parade, Fishponds 1912

A delightful view with children able to stand safely in the road. Cross Hands Hotel in the middle distance, standing at the junction for Downend and Staple Hill.

Today the Poplar trees have gone to make way for road widening, but the Cross Hands Hotel is still flourishing. New shops are behind the trees on the left. Note the number of road markings, a far cry from the top picture.

# Fishponds Road, Eastville, 1924

Looking towards Eastville Park, with Freemantle Road on the left and Berkeley Street on the right. The railway bridge carried the branch line connecting Clifton Down to Fishponds, Staple Hill, and Mangotsfield.

Today the bridge is gone, demolished in 1970, giving a pleasant view of Eastville Park at the junction of Fishponds Road and Muller Road.

# Stapleton Road from Eastville Park, 1906

Showing the original bridge over the Froom from Eastville Park, with the farm and the cluster of cottages around it. Note the group of trees including a pine on river bank near the bridge.

A new bridge was built over the Froom in 1929, just visible underneath the M32 flyover, which brings the M32 motorway into the centre of Bristol. The Merchants Arms Inn is situated beneath the motorway, with allotments by the river. Note the Post Office Tower on the slopes of Purdown.

# St. George 1913

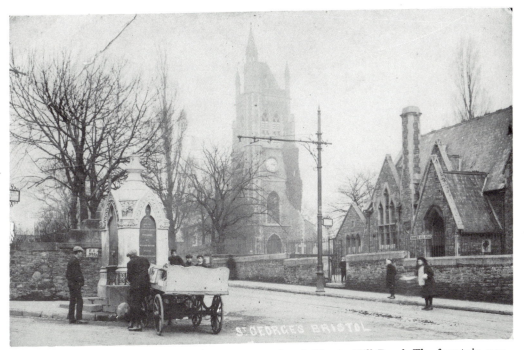

The fountain at the junction of Summerhill Road and Clouds Hill Road. The fountain was presented to the parishioners by William Butler of Clifton in 1889. Children showing great interest at the horse drinking from the water trough. St. George's Church, the latest of several churches built on that site, was built in 1880, and demolished in July 1976.

The fountain, now with the water trough full of plants, still stands at the junction to Kingswood. Modern flats now built on the site of St. George's church.

# Staple Hill 1916

The High Street looking towards Fishponds. Note the domed frontage of the cinema on the right. It would seem that all the local children once again knew that the photographer was about to take a picture.

The cinema has lost its dome, and the building is now used for Bingo. It is still a busy shopping area, though parking of cars is always a problem. Note the narrower double curb and patched roads, the result of many repairs!

# High Street, Hanham, 1914

Looking towards the old village, with the Pound Ebenezer Chapel in the centre. The tram was No. 200, from Hanham to Bushy Park via Old Market. Adverts on wall for Rowntrees and Cadburys, and Dewars Whisky.

The Pound Evenezer Chapel was demolished for road widening in 1962. A road entrance, house, and later a modern library replaced the old building on the left.

# The Clock Tower, Kingswood, 1928

The Clock Tower on the left is a landmark of Kingswood, erected to commemorate Queen Victoria's Diamond Jubilee (1897).

Today the Clock Tower is still telling the time for present day shoppers. Lloyds and National Westminster Banks can be seen on the left, with the shops on the right remaining little changed. During the summer months many attractive flower displays can be seen through the main streets of Kingswood.

# Downend 1926

A quiet view of the village, with small shops on the left, a rank of cottages, and the Horseshoe Inn on the right. The bus, run by B & S, is at its terminus, with the crew leaning against the vehicle taking a breather between journeys. Unique Scout Memorial in the centre of the picture.

Modern shops predominate, with only the Horseshoe Inn and the Boy Scout Memorial remaining to remind one of more leisurely days.

# Grosvenor Road, St. Pauls, 1923

Houses with small front gardens. Busy shops and public houses, with children able to play in the street and roadway.

Today the old shops have made way for modern flats, and a landscaped green area with trees.

# Stokes Croft 1920's

Looking towards Cheltenham Road, with Hillgrove Street on the left, and the junction of City Road to the right of the tram. Note W.W. Kemps the jewellers, and their clock with Greenwich Mean Time written on the face, with Douglas Motors opposite.

A mixture of Old and New, with attractive new buildings blending in with the old shops opposite. Clements the Tailors went in the early 1970's.

# Arley Chapel, Cotham 1908

The junction of Arley Hill and Cheltenham Road. The foundation stone for Arley Chapel was laid in May 1845, with the Chapel built mainly of Bath stone.

Arley Chapel is now the Polish Roman Catholic Church in Bristol. The houses on the right of Cheltenham Road have lost part of their gardens for road widening.

# Zetland Road Junction 1908

This was a busy junction with a tram terminus in Elton Road. Seen here with a Tram Driver's Hut in the road, which was also used to let passengers wait in. Tram No. 189 going up Gloucester Road en route to Ashley Down, while the other tram is going to Staple Hill. Also on the left of the view is a milkman delivering milk out of a churn on the back of a horse drawn cart.

Today the road layout is much the same, with shops still on right going up Gloucester Road. A large building has been built on corner of Elton Road, which used to be Burton's the Tailor's, but today is a large off licence.

# Horfield Common 1915

Sheep graze safely where Kellaway Avenue is now. The building seen on the left is Cox's Farm. Horfield Barrack's in middle distance were demolished in 1966.

The fence on the left of the picture replaces the row of trees from the earlier view. Built in 1921, Kellaway Avenue now crosses the Common. A modern house now stands on the site of Cox's Farm.

# Henleaze Lane 1905

Henleaze Lane.

The Library, Henle[...]

This was a quiet lane leading through to Southmead. Shows a horse drawn cart parked outside a row of cottages, which was approximately where the Post Office is today.

Today Henleaze Lane is known as Henleaze Road, with the cottages on the left now gone and shops built in their place. The buildings still recognisable today are the gabled house on the right, (Henley Grove Lodge), and the Methodist Church, on the left in the middle distance.

# High Street and Passage Road, Westbury, 1916

Ladies take their time crossing the road, as car AF 47 meanders around the corner behind them, with Sims Baker's shop on the right hand corner, next door to the Butchers shop.

The pavement on the left hand side has been re-aligned, and a modern house has been built centre of picture, with a few trees still surviving behind. The White Lion Public House is still trading on the corner of Passage Road.

# High Street, Shirehampton, 1933

*High Street, Shirehampton.*

Looking towards the green, with the shop on the left having a notice over the door 'Enquire within for Everything'. The motor bike and side car the only form of traffic.

Still a busy shopping street with the Lifeboat Inn on the right. The old houses, being part of the original village, can be seen facing the green.

# Ashley Road 1920

The days when Rogers Special Stout cost 2/6d (12½p) a dozen bottles, or 1/6d (7½p) for a dozen half bottles. Note that the two tram lines became one at this point, until it reached the junction of City Road and Stokes Croft.

All the buildings centre of picture were cleared in the early 1970's and replaced with flats and houses, the buildings on the left remain, but much of Grosvenor Road on the left hand side, from the junction of St. Nicholas Road, has now gone.

# Ashley Hill Station 1910

This tranquil scene must surely be one of the most changed. This picture was taken before Muller Road was built, with up to four well worn paths leading to the station. Note the children posing for the camera.

The station was closed to passenger traffic on 23rd November 1964. Muller Road with its houses can be seen middle right, with modern flats on the skyline and Shaldon Road on the far right of the picture. Today's H.S.T. 125 trains are a far cry from the G.W.R. Engine in the top picture.

# Ashley Down Road 1922

Looking towards Mullers Orphanage, shows a man with a performing bear, and two small boys watching with enjoyment.

Today the rank of houses are still retained on the left, with the gate leading to Sefton Park School. The old Glenfrome House, surrounded by modern houses, is on the right.

# New Road, Eastville 1924

l after Muller's Orphanage, before all the houses of
ried the railway line to Fishponds and Staple Hill.

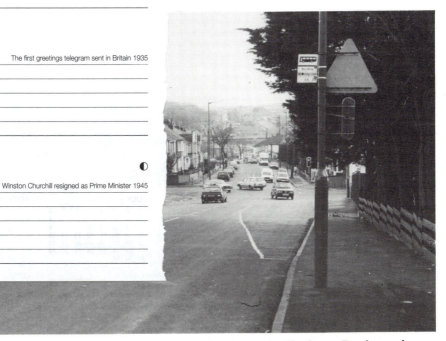

Today the road junction crossing the centre of the picture is Glenfrome Road, new houses
have been built. The trees of Eastville Park are visible on the skyline. The viaduct was
removed in 1968 to make way for the roundabout and M32.

# Muller Road 1926

Muller Road at the junction of Stapleton Road. The houses centre distance are newly built, with the fields of Purdown on the horizon.

The present day view is taken from the roundabout under the M32 looking up Muller Road. The trees to the left are where the new Eastgate Shopping Centre starts. The Iron Bridge over the river Froom is unchanged and can still be recognised.

# Filton 1918

Showing the Anchor Hotel with a walled field adjoining, used in the 1920's for camping by cyclists. The large sign advertises the Bristol Aeroplane Company, constructors of aircraft and aero engines, offices and works. Note the cobbled area and tram lines.

A large roundabout leads to the Anchor Hotel on the left, with Shield House formerly a laundry, now a technical college, on the right. Filton Church with modern spire can be seen in the distance, with the modern building of British Aerospace next to the hotel.

# Old Market 1930

Old Market Street in the early 1930's, looking from Midland Road towards the junction with Castle Street. Trams still in use and the tower of the Central Hall on the right.

Today in the centre distance can be seen the trees and open space of Castle Green Park, where bustling shops were in pre-1939. The shops on the right have been restored, preserving their original character.

# Trinity Church, St. Phillips, 1910

Trinity Church, perhaps on a Sunday morning, with people on the way to church, and the children in their Sunday best. Strangely not a tram in sight at this busy junction.

Today the church is Trinity Community Centre. The houses and shops on the right are gone, to make way for road widening, with modern flats, and other new development.

# Bath and Wells Road, Totterdown, 1911

Three Lamps junction. The signpost directs traffic to the lower road for Bath, and the upper road for Wells. On the signpost are Three Lamps, giving the junction its name.

The corner and shops, public houses and other buildings were all demolished in the early 1970's for road widening. The Three Lamps landmark is still directing traffic today, with the wall on the right of the picture still used for advertising boards today.

# Bath Road, 1911

The terraced houses, built of Bath stone, are opposite small flourishing shops, which include Hills Potato Merchants, and a Cycle and Motor Repair Garage. The slopes of Totterdown are on the horizon.

The little terraced houses and shops were pulled down for major road development in the 1970's. St. Phillips trading estate is off left of the picture, with the Turnpike Inn and the hills of Totterdown on the right.

# Wells Road, Totterdown, 1910

Looking towards Knowle, with the Y.M.C.A. on the corner, Lloyds Bank next door, and shops on both sides of the road. The cart, belonging to D.M.V. Bullock, is delivering mineral waters. Tram No. 70 winds its way down the hill.

The Y.M.C.A. corner still a feature today, with the modern Bush Inn on the left built on land cleared for road development. Private flats have replaced the shops on the right. Holy Nativity Church and some of the original shop fronts on the skyline.

# Wesleyan Chapel and Wells Road 1908

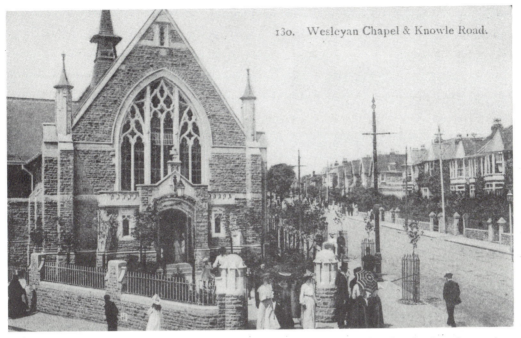

Sunday morning, a leisurely scene with the congregation leaving the church after the service. The trees are newly planted with protective railings.

The Methodist Church on the corner of Wells and Redcatch Roads, with the now mature trees lining the main road. Only the lamp over the door and the railings have changed.

# Wells Road, Knowle, 1924

Wells Road in about 1924, pictured here with early car and delivery carts, with the Talbot Hotel just beyond the Tram car stop.

Little has changed today in the layout of the road and buildings, except for the building of the Broadwalk Shopping Centre on the right. The Talbot public house still remains the same today. Knowle Post Office is in the same place as it was in 1924 but now with two post boxes on the pavement.

# Whitchurch Village 1905

The Village, Whitchurch.

Whitchurch was a quiet country village, with children playing in the road. Quite a large area to the right devoted to bill boards.

Whitchurch is now an area of Bristol and no longer a village. It lies on the main A37 Wells Road. The Black Lion Public House has kept its name, although a new building was built in place of the original, and set back from the road to leave space for a car park.

# Brislington 1915

The square, with the Post Office using part of the large house, the Grocer and Tea Dealer next door and many advert hoardings, including Brooks Dry Cleaners and Fry's Cocoa. Note the small Chapel.

All the properties including the Post Office now gone, with the start of modern shop developments on the right, which extends up the left side of Brislington Hill. The houses behind the trees survive today, at the corner of Church Parade.

# Sandy Park Road, Brislington, approximately 1914

A rather quiet road compared with today. Pavement parking for two horse carts, the owners perhaps participating in a tipple in the Sandringham Public House. Note Brooks the Cleaners on the left, and Hodders the Chemist on the right, two famous Bristol business names from the past.

The wrought iron sign on top of the Sandringham has long since gone, along with the old lamp above the door. The pavement parking is now done by cars. The tree centre distance has survived both time and gales.

# INDEX

# ACKNOWLEDGEMENT

Our thanks to Mr. Ted Houghton for his interest and advice.

ISBN 0 9514648 0 9